MESSAGE ON A PLATE

Laurent Bize

Balboa Press books may be ordered through booksellers or by contacting:

Balboa Press
A Division of Hay House
1663 Liberty Drive
Bloomington, IN 47403
www.balboapress.com
1 (877) 407-4847

Because of the dynamic nature of the Internet, any web addresses or links contained in this book may have changed since publication and may no longer be valid. The views expressed in this work are solely those of the author and do not necessarily reflect the views of the publisher, and the publisher hereby disclaims any responsibility for them.

Any people depicted in stock imagery provided by Thinkstock are models, and such images are being used for illustrative purposes only.
Certain stock imagery © Thinkstock.

ISBN: 978-1-5043-3586-7 (sc)
ISBN: 978-1-5043-3587-4 (e)

Library of Congress Control Number: 2015910695

Print information available on the last page.

Balboa Press rev. date: 7/16/2015

BALBOA
PRESS
A DIVISION OF HAY HOUSE

For Every ONE

Contents

Foreword
James Twyman

The message of today, whether regarding spirituality or health, is integration. How do we understand the value and importance of positive, healthy living in relation to everything we know about spirituality and nutrition? This book does just that in a unique, interesting way. *Message on a Plate* focuses on one of the most common staples in the modern meal: the natural, earthy and always diverse world of the salad.

Laurent's masterpiece, the first of its kind, combines the colour meaning of food ingredients with their corresponding chakras. Stop just one moment – did you really get what you just read? A salad corresponding with the ancient knowledge of the chakra system? That's exactly what you're about to read: a collection of easily put-together recipes designed to uplift the mind, body and soul.

The energy and love that has gone into this book pour forth from its pages, and its beautiful illustrations will both delight and inspire you into wanting to try each and every dish. Know that you are eating healthy food, whilst nourishing and invigorating your energy centres.

This book offers an easy way to practice this wisdom on a daily basis and provide beneficial impact on the psychological, meditative, spiritual and of course, physical well-being of everyone who commits to this study. In short, the simplest expression of a healthy meal, the meal just became a wellspring of spiritual and esoteric wisdom.

Give yourself the gift of entering the world of salad creativity and discover how to treat yourself and your loved ones with spiritual nourishment and well-being.

A new world is about to open up for you …

James Twyman
New York Times bestselling author of *The Moses Code* and *Emissary of Light*

Acknowledgements

My children deserve my deepest acknowledgement for experimenting with me on many of the dishes in this book. Though they were unaware, both of them have helped me to be imaginative with the produce I use and create colourful presentation platters to encourage them to joyfully eat fresh, tasty and healthy meals that include various fruits and vegetables.

A great thanks to all my special friends in England and France who gave me the opportunity to prepare these dishes for them in their homes and mine. They gave me that extra ingredient: love. Thanks to their great company and conversation, I was inspired to compile these exquisite recipes.

I would like to give special mention to the most caring, loving, understanding and beautiful love partner of mine, Karen. She offered me space as well as support during the critical stage of reviewing and editing the manuscript. She also reminded me of the importance of finding the right balance between work and play by practicing the art of moderation in everything we do. She is a great source of inspiration for the compilation of the dishes I created whilst thinking of her. I hope to share these with you in this book, along with further delightful recipes and ingredients.

I thank you, reader, for being inspired to purchase *Message on a Plate* and to favour this type of eating, with a willingness to remove any processed food from your diet for you and your loved ones as often as the opportunity presents itself. I came to realise that it is far cheaper to cook with fresh ingredients than to buy ready-made meals. The added bonus is that you know what you are feeding your 'temple'. These recipes do not take much more time to prepare, and they will provide you with great satisfaction.

Finally, I would like to thank my worldwide friends from 'Generation 1' and beyond, as well as my mum, for their support, encouragement, and wisdom over the past year. A particular mention and sincere gratitude go to Korkarn from Thailand and Gonul from Turkey. They provided me with the motivation and idea to create this book. They saw the simplicity in it, they held the vision of it as a great concept, they took time to review and advise on the recipes, they challenged me when I needed it and they gave me the spark to see the chakra connection and hear the energy message that each fruit, vegetable, salad and herb unfolds within us, once we wish to embrace it.

I am blessed!

Introduction

Fruits and vegetables, herbs and salads are talking to us! Every day!

The concept came to me when I started to observe my eating choices and habits and came across the book *The Colours Speak* by William Berton. With intuition, I began to relate to the messages contained in vegetarian produce.

The produce is speaking to us – communicating through amazing colours, beautiful smells, refreshing and delicious textures. Each item embraces a specific message ready to be imparted. The many combinations are a treat for the eyes and taste buds and enlightens the mind.

Many of you have heard of the benefit of eating five portions of fruit and vegetables a day. I believe that you, your children, your family and your friends will eat at least ten portions a day once you discover the meaning of each fruit and vegetable and understand its language. These delights are pure creations of love from the earth and sun to provide our bodies with the vital nutrients they need to live the best all-around healthy life. They boost the immune system as well as enhancing the vibrations and colours of our chakras.

Remember the expression 'You are what you eat'? You will come to learn through this book the true meaning behind this quote. You will be endowed with clarity, inspiration and energy every day – every time you eat breakfast, lunch and dinner.

The recipes in this book take little time to prepare. I hope they will inspire you to embrace the magic of cooking and connect with your inner creativity.

It will be a pleasure and a daily ritual for you to prepare, eat, and perhaps even cultivate wondrous, nourishing food. The dishes and their meaning will give you a completely different perspective on your life and well-being.

The various salads and recipes presented here are very easy to create. Each is composed of locally found, common, everyday ingredients available in all food markets and shops and is more affordable than ready-made meals or processed food, especially when purchased in season. I would recommend favouring organic produce, as these fruits and vegetables are grown in a more natural way with respect to the environment. Look also for local produce, as it will be fresher than any imported product. However, exotic produce also has great benefits and flavours.

Thank you for purchasing this book. I wish you a lot of joy and happiness travelling and experimenting with its contents!

Preparation of the dishes

For the best result, prepare all the ingredients prior to creating the dish. Once the ingredients are cut, display them in front of you, either on your cutting board or in small containers. The *mise en place,* or preparation stage with a neat and clean worktop, are key to assembling the recipe with ease. The quantity of the ingredients listed in each recipe will comfortably make two servings. You will need to halve the quantity to create one plate. You can also refer to the picture to guide you

Message of the dishes

You will notice some words are in *italic* in each of the recipes. These words correspond to the meaning of the ingredients and represent the vibrational element of the produce used in the dish. You can also refer to each meaning by looking at the section 'A to Z Guide to Fruits and Vegetables: Meanings, Vibration and Related Chakras'.

Health advice

The recipes promote meals that provide more balance of alkaline vs. acidity in the body. Many processed foods, as well as meat and fish products, are contributing towards an acidic diet and can cause many disruptions to the body when over-consumed. Conversely, making time to prepare your meal with fresh ingredients containing 70 per cent vegetarian produce every day, may turn your diet more towards alkaline balance and help you keep away, as well as reduce drastically, all kinds of diseases and ailments. You will feel lighter, healthier and revitalised!

This book is intended as an introductory, informational guide to general well-being techniques and is not meant to treat, diagnose or prescribe. The tools described herein are not for the purpose of replacing standard-of-care treatment prescribed by healthcare professionals. Neither the author, nor the publisher, accepts any responsibility for your health or how you choose to use the information contained in this book.

The Collection in Pictures

The concept

We are surrounded by colour – we live in a kaleidoscope of colours – and yet we often take colours for granted. Did you know that colours influence us to the very core of ourselves? Colour is the centre of life. Colour affects our state of mind and choices, encourages the way we respond to situations or people and makes our feelings profound without us even realising it. Thankfully, the colours in fruits and vegetables allow us to receive their energy and vibration with total satisfaction and confidence, due to their brightness, taste and usefulness.

Colour therapy helps on a physical, as well as a psychological and spiritual basis. Many holistic practitioners are encouraging patients to delve into this subject because colour addresses all levels of our being. Every fruit and vegetable is a gift of nature. This reason alone provides produce with the power to work in unison with our bodies, with each fruit and vegetable having a meaning that stimulates the body and mind.

Based on these principles, each fruit and vegetable has its own language. A mix of ingredients presents you with a unique and inspiring message to reflect upon whilst preparing, eating and engaging the dishes with your six senses. See, touch, smell, hear, feel and connect with your meal as if you were listening to a symphony. Learn to embrace the energy it produces within you. Utter bliss!

Follow your intuition when buying fruits and vegetables. Once home and ready to start, give the produce a blessing whilst washing it under water. Follow with a grateful intention prior to the preparation process and when your creation is ready to be eaten.

Be your own guide. Substitute, add or remove an ingredient from any of the recipes if you like, knowing that the outcome will be perfect for you and your family. You can relate to the meaning of each ingredient chosen and eaten on its own and understand the benefit it brings to you and how that can be related to multiple situations in your life. Let your inner inspiration take over.

I have created these recipes using this same method. The pleasure and feel-good factor multiplies when I share a meal with family and friends and it often turns out to be an enlightening topic of conversation at the dinner table.

I feel privileged to have been given the opportunity to publish and share this knowledge for the benefit of everyone. Enjoy the journey and the taste.

Bon appétit!

Chakras constitute our 'wheel of light'. The ancient healers from India and China some 2,600 years ago described chakras as our centres to take and distribute energies from the outside, as well as from the inside of our body. Each one is associated with our physical, mental and emotional state and is situated in one of the seven endocrine glands that are interlaced throughout our body and interrelated. Chakras are the subtle and powerful frequency centres of our energy system.

We can see and feel our chakras through our health, stamina, mood and thoughts. The more we balance, clear and expand our chakras, the better the enhancement of our different states of being. We can do this in many ways: through meditation, colour or sound therapies, but also by connecting with the wonder Mother Earth provides us when preparing and eating fruits and vegetables.

The symbolic meaning of each chakra is summarised in one or two words and composes the collective of ourselves:

- *body* for the root chakra
- *emotion* for the sacral chakra
- *mind* for the solar-plexus chakra
- *unconditional love* for the heart chakra
- *expression* for the throat chakra
- *imagination* for the third-eye chakra
- *connection* for the crown chakra

Combine the colour meaning with the corresponding chakra, focusing your attention on its location and feel the vibration throughout your body when preparing and eating these freshly made dishes. Embrace the significance to your daily life and situation. Stay focused, uplifted and filled with high spirits. Let the sensations and energies rise around and inside you and the transcript of the message transform into pure reality for you.

This is neither a scientific experiment, nor an answer to resolve all of life's challenges. It is a simple and empowering way to balance our energies; improve our mental, emotional and physical health and connect with the beauty and grace of the living source on earth.

The composition of any of these dishes will inspire you with a positive message and will enhance these energy centres, as well as provide you with delightful pleasure and surprises. You might even achieve the body weight you have always wanted without the need for dieting.

That is my wish for you!

The seven main chakras
Colours, Locations, Function, Abilities

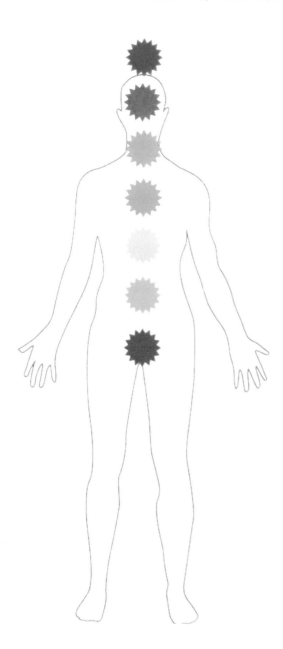

VIOLET – CROWN CHAKRA
Function: Personal identification with infinite
Abilities: Being, Oneness, Wisdom

INDIGO – THIRD EYE CHAKRA
Function: Channel intuition & clear perception
Abilities: Insight, Imagination, Depth

BLUE – THROAT CHAKRA
Function: Communication
Abilities: Creativity, Clarification, Expression

GREEN – HEART CHAKRA
Function: Love & understanding
Abilities: Compassion, Empathy, Connection

YELLOW – SOLAR PLEXUS CHAKRA
Function: Power & will
Abilities: Self-control, Discipline, Intellect

ORANGE – SACRAL CHAKRA
Function: Emotions & feelings
Abilities: Exploration, Desire, Devotion

RED – ROOT CHAKRA
Function: Ground spirit force in body
Abilities: Health, Security, Power, Wealth

VEGETARIAN AND CHEESE PLATES

Majestic – *Majestueux*

Duo of asparagus and avocado mixed with fresh arugula leaves and garden peas and dressed with a mixture of honey-coated gooseberries, parsley and walnut oil

> ## The Message:
>
> You are in *alignment* with *knowledge* and *modesty*. Feel the *cleansing* taking place. It brings you and others *abundance* and *fluidity* in life. You are filled with *optimism* towards all your actions and thoughts.

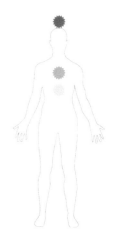

Ingredients

- 10 asparagus spears
- 200 grams arugula leaves
- 100 grams fresh peas
- 2 soup spoons walnut oil
- 10 gooseberries, cut into quarters
- 4 stems of fresh parsley, chopped
- 4 tea spoons honey
- 1 avocado, sliced

Preparation

1. Blanch the asparagus for 8 minutes in boiling water. Let cool before placing on a plate. Top with the arugula leaves.
2. Blanch the fresh peas for 4 minutes in boiling water. Let cool before adding to the plate.
3. Prepare the dressing: Heat the walnut oil in a saucepan. Add the gooseberries and cook until softened, about 2 minutes. Remove from the heat. Add the parsley and honey.
4. Fan the avocado slices and place in the middle of the plate.
5. Sprinkle the dressing all around and serve.

Colours in Harmony – *Harmonie en Couleurs*

A wedding of yellow and orange peppers with aubergine (eggplant) and courgette (zucchini), enhanced with red onion and fresh tarragon, placed on a bed of little gem lettuce and coated with a string of honey

The Message:

You have the *proficiency* to feel *enlightened vibration*. Make *available* your *abilities* and personal *expression* for *kindness* towards others throughout the day.

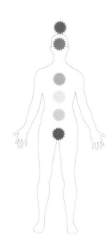

Ingredients

- 2 soup spoons olive oil
- 1 small aubergine, sliced into rectangles, skin on
- 1 courgette, sliced into rectangles, skin on
- 1 yellow pepper, sliced into medium strips
- 1 orange pepper, sliced into medium strips
- 1 red onion, thinly sliced
- 1 tomato, cut into eighths
- sea salt to taste
- ground pepper to taste
- 2 heads little gem lettuce, sliced
- 2 stems of tarragon, chopped leaves
- 2 tea spoons clear honey

Preparation

1. Heat the oil in a pan. Add the aubergine and simmer for 5 minutes. Add the courgette, peppers, onion and tomato. Sprinkle with salt and pepper. Cover with a lid and cook, stirring occasionally, for 8 minutes. Remove from the heat.
2. Arrange the lettuce on a plate. Top with the cooked vegetable mixture. Add the tarragon and drizzle the honey all over and serve.

Experiment – *Experience*

Medley of pink lady apples, celery, sweetcorn and romaine lettuce, enhanced with extra mature Cheddar, flavoured with dried cranberries, pumpkin seeds, almonds, walnuts and red onion, mixed with a wholegrain mustard dressing and chives

The Message:

You are *flexible* today. Your *inner truth* brings *clarity* and *balance*, *optimising* your *abilities*. *Welcome* and *harvest* the *quality* of your *contribution* to the world.

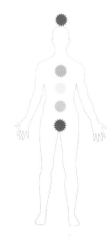

Ingredients

- 1 cob sweetcorn, cut lengthways once cooked
- 1 red onion, thinly sliced
- 2 celery sticks, thinly sliced
- 40 grams Cheddar cheese, diced
- 50 grams dried cranberries
- 6 walnuts, broken
- 10 almonds, broken
- 20 pumpkin seeds
- 1 tea spoon wholegrain mustard
- 4 soup spoons walnut oil
- salt & pepper to taste
- 2 soup spoon cider vinegar
- 1 head romaine lettuce, shredded
- 1 pink lady apple, sliced into triangles
- 15 chives, chopped
- 3 pieces of toast or bread, for garnish

Preparation

1. Place the corn cob into boiling water for 6 minutes. Let cool.
2. Cut the corn lengthways and put in a large bowl along with the onion, celery, cheese, cranberries, walnuts, almonds and pumpkin seeds.
3. In a bowl, combine in the following order the mustard, walnut oil, salt and pepper. Add the vinegar and mix until the dressing reaches a smooth consistency.
4. Add the lettuce and apple to the corn mixture. Pour the dressing all over and mix well.
5. Arrange on plates and garnish with chopped chives, toast or bread.

Glittering Star – *Etoile Scintillante*

White endive and oak leaf lettuce, dancing with burst walnuts, hazelnuts, sliced red and green apples, aged Cheddar and blue cheese, crowned with grapes and apricot

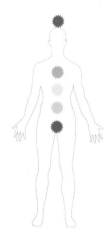

The Message:

Your *wisdom* and *optimism* enhance your *health*, generating *happiness* and *joy*. With *passion*, you *contemplate* your *spiritual wealth* expanding.

Ingredients

- 1 head oak leaf lettuce, shredded
- 1 white endive, thinly sliced
- 8 grapes, cut into quarters
- 1 red apple, cut into small triangles
- 1 green apple, cut into small triangles
- 1 apricot, sliced into segments
- 30 grams Cheddar cheese, diced
- 30 grams blue cheese, diced
- 6 hazelnuts, crushed
- 6 walnuts, crushed
- thin slices of spring onion (optional)
- 2 soup spoons walnut oil
- freshly-ground black pepper to taste

Preparation

1. Combine the lettuce and endive and place in the centre of a plate. Arrange the grapes on top.
2. Slice the apples and apricot into half-moon and triangle shapes. Arrange on the salad.
3. Sprinkle the cheeses, hazelnuts and walnuts over the salad. Add onion slices if you wish.
4. Sprinkle the salad with walnut oil. Finish with freshly-ground black pepper.

Celebration – *Celebration*

Dancing cantaloupe melon and pink grapefruit, with curly leaves, singing with sugar snap peas and spring onions, sprinkled with pumpkin seeds, spiced with red chilli, honey, sesame oil and cracked black pepper

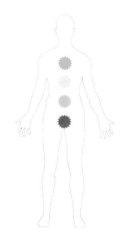

The Message:

Conviviality and *spontaneity*
tap into your natural
youth energy to *attract*
ease and *clarity* of life.

Ingredients

- 1 head curly lettuce
- 14 sugar snap peas, blanched
- 1/3 cantaloupe melon, halved and sliced into 16 equal portions
- 1 pink grapefruit, separated into segments, juice reserved
- 1 large spring onion, sliced into rings
- 1 red chilli, halved, pips removed and cut into thin rectangles
- 40 pumpkin seeds
- 2 tea spoons honey
- 2 soup spoons sesame oil
- cracked black pepper to taste

Preparation

1. Display the lettuce on a plate.
2. Blanch the sugar snap peas for 3 minutes in boiling water. Cool and display atop the lettuce.
3. Arrange the melon, grapefruit, onion and chilli on the plate. Splash with the grapefruit juice.
4. Sprinkle the pumpkin seeds over the salad.
5. Slowly dip a tea spoon into a jar of honey. Drizzle a thin length in circles all over the salad. Repeat. Sprinkle the sesame oil on top. Sprinkle with the pepper and serve.

Constellation – *Constellation*

Blue and goat cheese, dressed with sweet potatoes and broccoli florets, resting on a duo of endive and little gem lettuce, enlightened with cashew nuts, sprinkled with cream dressing

The Message:

Your *enthusiasm* creates *kindness* to others, *offering* a day filled with *wisdom* and *grace*.

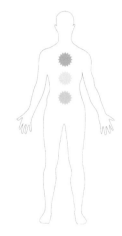

Ingredients

- 10 broccoli florets, prepared
- 2 medium sweet potatoes, peeled and cut into squares
- 1 head little gem lettuce, thinly sliced
- 1 yellow endive, thinly sliced
- 40 grams blue cheese, diced
- 40 grams goat cheese, diced
- 20 cashew nuts, whole
- 60 millilitres single cream
- black pepper to taste
- 1 or 2 soup spoons cider vinegar

Preparation

1. Bring water to the boil in a saucepan. Add the broccoli and potatoes and cook for 6 minutes. Remove from the heat and cool down with cold water.
2. Place the lettuce and endive in the centre of a plate. Top with the cooked potatoes and broccoli. Sprinkle with the cheeses and display the cashews.
3. In a bowl, mix the cream, pepper and the vinegar. Sprinkle all over the salad and serve.

Enlightenment – *Lumiere*

Refreshing medley of carrot, radishes, red pepper, peas and fine beans radiating in harmony with arugula leaves and shining with coriander, red onion and mustard dressing

The Message:

Your *ability* to be *sensitive* and *empathic* towards others still allows you to stay in *alignment* with your soul. Let this *warmth* and *trustworthiness* bring *abundance* and *vitality* within you.

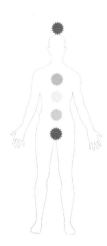

Ingredients

- 100 grams fine beans
- 100 grams arugula salad
- 8 radishes, cut into quarters
- 1 large carrot, cut into fine batons
- 32 fresh single peas removed from the pod
- 1/4 red pepper, diced into small cubes
- 1 red onion, peeled and cut lengthways into whole fine slices
- 8 coriander leaves
- 1 tea spoon mustard
- 4 soup spoons olive oil
- 2 soup spoons white wine vinegar

Preparation

1. Blanch the beans in hot water for 10 minutes.
2. Place the arugula in the centre of a plate joining your hands together to create volume. Arrange the radishes, carrot, peas, pepper, onion, coriander and cooked beans evenly around and on top of the leaves.
3. In a bowl, combine in the following order, the mustard, salt, pepper and olive oil. Mix together then add the vinegar and mix well to obtain a smooth consistency. Sprinkle on top of the salad and serve.

Water Lily – *Nenuphare*

Circle of courgette (zucchini) with minted couscous, garnished with red and yellow peppers, cherry tomatoes, enhanced with red onion, raisins, fennel and sprinkled with parsley

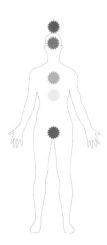

The Message:

Through your *perseverance* and *intuition*, you have the *warm presence* to *cleanse* your thoughts and make *available* your *abilities* to reach the *loveliness* of *enlightenment*.

Ingredients

- 300g couscous
- 40 grams butter
- 30g mint, chopped
- 40 grams raisins, soaked in hot water
- 1 red onion, chopped
- 1 red pepper, diced
- 1 yellow pepper, diced
- 10 cherry tomatoes, cut into quarters
- 2 soup spoons olive oil
- 500 millimetres water
- 1 courgette, diced
- 1 head fennel, chopped
- 4 stems of parsley, chopped

Preparation

1. Boil the water in a pan. Remove from the heat and add the couscous, butter and mint. Cover and let it stand for 6 to 8 minutes. Drain off any excess of water. Stir well with a fork and place in a bowl with the raisins, onion, peppers and tomatoes and 1 soup spoon of olive oil.
2. Heat 1 soup spoon of olive oil in the pan. Add the fennel, gently cook for a few minutes until softened. Transfer the fennel to the bowl with the couscous and mix.
3. In the same pan, add the courgette and turn them when golden. Remove from the heat and the pan when tender.
4. Place the courgette onto plates and arrange the couscous in the middle. Sprinkle with the parsley and serve.

Note: This dish can serve 4 and is delicious hot or cold. It tastes even nicer when you leave the couscous for one day in the fridge.

Tree of Life - *Arbre de Vie*

Duo of olives with cherry tomatoes, cucumber and fennel enlaced with red onion, Batavia lettuce and parsley, topped with feta cheese and olive oil

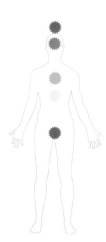

The Message:

Trust your *abilities*! Through *perseverance* and *visualisation* you *embody freedom*. Your *compassion* and *loveliness* towards others *cleanses* the world.

Ingredients

- 1 head Batavia lettuce, chopped
- 1/2 cucumber, sliced
- 10 cherry tomatoes, cut into quarters
- 1 red onion, thinly sliced
- 1/2 head fennel, thinly sliced
- 10 black olives, sliced into rings
- 10 green olives, sliced into rings
- 40 grams feta cheese, diced
- chopped parsley, for garnish
- 4 soup spoons olive oil
- black pepper to taste (optional)

Preparation

1. Place the lettuce in the centre of a plate. Arrange the cucumber on top, then the cherry tomatoes (reserving a few quarters), then the onion, fennel and the olives.
2. Sprinkle the cheese over the salad. Add a few tomato and cucumber quarters to the middle. Garnish with chopped parsley.
3. Sprinkle the salad with olive oil. Grind some black pepper on top if you wish and serve.

Mandala of Joy – *Mandala de Joie*

Trio of red potatoes, leek slices and cherry tomatoes, pan-fried with rosemary and shallots, surrounded with white grapes and beetroot, sprinkled with coriander

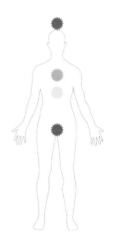

The Message:

With *patience* and *perseverance*, you *heal* everyone around you, *creating a new mastery* within all to activate global *empathy* and *friendliness*.

Ingredients

- 2 soup spoons olive oil, plus more for sprinkling
- 6 medium red potatoes, diced
- salt to taste
- pepper to taste
- 1 leek, sliced
- 20g coriander, chopped
- 20g rosemary, chopped
- 2 shallots, sliced
- 1/2 head fennel, chopped
- 7 cherry tomatoes, whole
- 14 white grapes, sliced
- 1 raw beetroot, sliced then halved

Preparation

1. Heat the 2 soup spoons of oil in a pan. Add the potatoes and cook, shaking well until slightly browned, around 10 to 15 minutes.
2. Season the potatoes with salt and pepper and add the leek, rosemary, shallots and fennel. Cover to let the ingredients cook and infuse together.
3. Stir the vegetables well until the flavour rises. Add the cherry tomatoes and cook for 2 to 3 minutes more.
4. Remove from heat, mix in the coriander and arrange the salad on a plate. Garnish with the grapes and beetroot. Sprinkle some olive oil around the edge if you wish.

FISH AND SEAFOOD PLATES

Light Caress – *Caresse Lumineuse*

Duo of oak leaf and round lettuce sprinkled with fresh peas, lemon and crushed walnuts, garnished with salmon fillets, sliced tomato and white onion, dancing with blood-orange segments, basil and olive oil

The Message:

Contemplate the *fineness* and *freshness* of the *light. Trust* the *rhapsody* of life to give *birth* to *abundance* and *stimulate* your *decisions.*

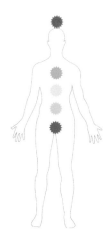

Ingredients

- 2 salmon fillets (150-200 grams each)
- sea salt to taste
- cracked black pepper to taste
- 30 grams single peas, removed from pod
- 1/4 head oak leaf lettuce, separated
- 1/4 head round lettuce, cut
- 1 blood orange, separated into segments
- 1 tomato, sliced
- 1 white onion, sliced
- 10 basil leaves, chopped
- 6 walnuts, crushed
- 4 soup spoons olive oil
- squeeze of lemon juice

Preparation

1. Preheat the oven to 180 degrees.
2. Sprinkle the salmon fillets with sea salt and cracked black pepper.
3. Cook the salmon in the oven (no oil) for 12 to 15 minutes, or to your taste.
4. Blanch the peas for 2 minutes in boiling water (uncooked is fine also).
5. Place the lettuce leaves onto a plate evenly. Top with the salmon. Arrange the orange segments, the tomato and onion slices around the salmon. Sprinkle with the basil and walnuts. Finish with a drizzle of olive oil and a squeeze of lemon juice. Serve with additional cracked pepper if desired.

Love Temple – *Temple d'Amour*

Fresh spinach and cucumber garnished with freshwater prawns, elevated by a trio of orange, lime and lemon segments, sprinkled with fresh tarragon and white onion, flavoured with sesame oil and ground black pepper

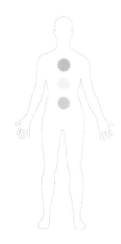

The Message:

Embody the *vibration* of the *light* with *determination* to *fuse* the *sensation* of a new *birth* towards life *appreciation*.

Ingredients

- 200 grams spinach, washed
- 1/4 cucumber, sliced into halves
- 1 orange, separated into segments
- 1 lime, separated into segments
- 1 lemon, separated into segments
- 100 grams prawns in brine, drained
- 1 white onion, thinly sliced
- 2 stems of tarragon, leaves removed and stems discarded
- 2 or 4 soup spoons sesame oil to taste
- ground black pepper to taste

Preparation

1. Arrange some spinach leaves on a plate. Display the cucumber halves on the plate. Rotate the orange, lime and lemon segments on the spinach. Place the prawns in the centre of the salad. Sprinkle with the onion slices and tarragon leaves.
2. Pour the sesame oil around the salad. Grind black pepper on top.

Direction – *Direction*

Poached Scottish smoked haddock, leading a trio of arugula, Chinese leaf and oak leaf lettuce, with sweet potato showing the way, along with pan-fried ginger, fennel, lemon, red onion and chives on top

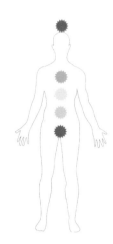

The Message:

Welcome with *enthusiasm* the *belief* and *willingness* to be *aligned* with your actions. It will provide you with the *ability* to *contemplate* the *loveliness* of the *light* within you.

Ingredients

- 2 pieces smoked haddock (150 grams each)
- 500 millilitre milk (or soya milk)
- 1 large sweet potato, sliced
- 2 soup spoons olive oil
- 1 red onion, thinly sliced
- 1 head fennel, thinly sliced sideways
- 10 grams ginger, diced
- 100 grams arugula salad
- 1/4 head Chinese leaf lettuce, cut
- 1/4 head oak leaf lettuce, cut
- squeeze of lemon juice
- 4 chives, whole

Preparation

1. Cook the haddock for 7 minutes in boiling water (or milk/soya milk).
2. Cook the sliced sweet potato for 7 minutes in boiling water and let cool.
3. Heat some olive oil in a pan and when hot, cook the onion, fennel and ginger for 4 minutes.
4. Display the lettuce leaves on a plate. Arrange the sweet-potato slices on top. Place the haddock in the middle of the salad. Top with the onion mixture and the squeezed lemon.
5. Add a touch of olive oil all around if desired. Finish with the chives and serve.

Big Bang - *Big Bang*

Oak leaf lettuce and fine beans with boiled white potatoes and egg, enhanced with green and black olives, white onion and tomato, topped with anchovies and coarse-grain mustard dressing

The Message:

Visualise and *contemplate* the *birth* of your latest *decisions*. They are the *discipline* of both your *sensibility* and *compassion.*

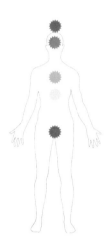

Ingredients

- 2 medium white potatoes, cut into quarters
- 150 grams fine beans
- 1 egg
- 1/4 head oak leaf lettuce
- 12 black olives
- 12 green olives
- 1 tomato, cut into eighths
- 100 grams fresh anchovies in oil
- 1 white onion, thinly sliced
- 1 tea spoon coarse-grain mustard
- 6 soup spoons olive oil
- 2 soup spoon white wine vinegar

Preparation

1. Put the potatoes in a pan filled with cold water. Turn up the heat and once the water boils, check the potatoes and remove when ready.
2. Add the beans to the boiling water and cook for 10 minutes. Remove and allow to cool.
3. Plunge the egg in boiling water and cook for 10 minutes. Cool, remove the shell and cut into 6 equal segments.
4. Arrange the lettuce on the plate. Scatter the potatoes on the lettuce. Add the beans, olives and tomato. Add the egg. Top with the fresh anchovies in oil. Scatter the onion on top.
5. In a bowl, combine the mustard with the olive oil and a pinch of salt and pepper. Add the vinegar and mix well to obtain a smooth consistency. Sprinkle over the salad and serve.

Amazement – *Emerveillement*

Pan-fried king prawns, with garlic butter and shallots, resting on a fan of avocado atop Chinese leaves, sprinkled with peas, circled with satsuma segments and topped with lemon wedges

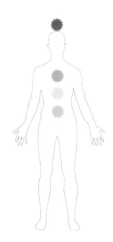

The Message:

The *dynamism* of your *light* within gives you the *knowledge* to *practice patience* and generate *abundant* acts of *kindness* towards yourself and others.

Ingredients

- 100 grams podded peas
- 2 soup spoons olive oil
- 10 king prawns, shelled
- 1 shallot, thinly chopped
- 2 garlic cloves, thinly chopped
- 30 grams butter
- 1/4 head Chinese leaf lettuce, sliced
- 2 satsumas, peeled and separated into segments
- 1 avocado, peeled and sliced
- 1 lemon, cut into wedges

Preparation

1. Blanch the peas for 2 minutes in boiling water and let cool.
2. Heat the olive oil in a pan and add the prawns with the shallots. Cook until they change colour on one side. Add the garlic, turn the shrimp over and simmer for 2 to 3 minutes over a medium heat. Remove from the heat and melt the butter in the pan.
3. Arrange the lettuce in the middle of a plate. Arrange the satsuma segments around the leaves. Rotate the avocado on the plate. Top with the prawns and sprinkle on the peas.
4. Dress the salad with the shallots, garlic and melted butter. Top with the lemon wedges.

Fulfilment – *Epanouissement*

Grilled swordfish steak flavoured with thyme and shallots, lying on Chinese leaves and fine beans, enlaced with boiled potatoes and a duo of olives, enlightened with tomato, sprinkled with walnut oil and balsamic vinegar

The Message:

Attune your *sensibility* towards *compassion*. This *discipline attracts patience* and *optimism* within, allowing you to *visualise* and *decide* your actions.

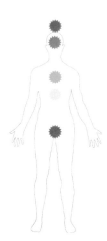

Ingredients

- 6 small potatoes
- 100 grams fine beans
- 1/4 head Chinese leaf lettuce, sliced
- 2 swordfish steaks (200 grams each)
- 2 shallots, thinly sliced
- 2 tomatoes, cut into eighths and then into sixteenths
- 8 black olives, thinly sliced
- 8 green olives, thinly sliced
- 4 stems of thyme, chopped
- 4 or 6 soup spoons walnut oil to taste
- 1 or 2 tea spoons balsamic vinegar to taste

Preparation

1. Put the potatoes in a pan filled with cold water. Turn up the heat and once the water boils, check the potatoes and remove when ready. Cool and cut into twelfths.
2. Add the beans to the boiling water and cook for 10 minutes and allow to cool.
3. In the meantime, place the lettuce on a plate.
4. Heat a grill pan (or frying pan) Once the pan is hot, add the swordfish and cook for 2 minutes each side, or until the steaks start to sweat (no oil needed).
5. Arrange the potatoes, beans, shallots, tomatoes, olives and thyme on the bed of the lettuce. Top with the swordfish.
6. Drizzle with walnut oil and vinegar before serving.

Light Within – *Lumiere Interieur*

Duo of pear and avocado, enhanced with arugula salad and crayfish, with satsuma segments, sprinkled with crushed almonds and walnut oil

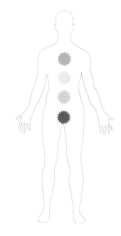

The Message:

Your *inner truth* brings you the *knowledge* to be *aligned* and generates the *dynamism* towards the *optimism* of *securing* your dreams.

Ingredients

- 60 grams arugula salad
- 2 satsumas, peeled and separated into segments
- 1 pear, sliced
- 1 avocado, sliced
- 100 grams net crayfish in brine, drained
- 2 almonds, crushed
- 4 soup spoons walnut oil

Preparation

1. Place the arugula salad in the centre of the plate. Display the satsuma segments.
2. Fan some of the pear and avocado slices and display on the plate, alternating. Cut the remainder in small pieces and add to the salad. Top with the crayfish.
3. Scatter the almonds over the salad, drizzle with walnut oil and serve.

Propulsion – *Propulsion*

Smoked salmon flowers flirting with avocado and white grapefruit by a lamb-lettuce heart, topped with spring onions and red chillies, enhanced with cream and chives

The Message:

With *calm* and *ease, welcome* the *knowledge* and *assertiveness* of the *youth* within you.

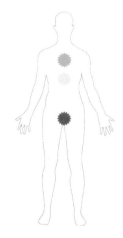

Ingredients

- 200 grams smoked salmon (6 slices)
- 30 grams lamb lettuce
- 1 avocado, quartered
- 1 white grapefruit, separated into segments, juice reserved
- 2 spring onions, thinly sliced
- 2 red chillies, thinly sliced
- 80 millilitres single cream
- black pepper to taste
- chives, cut into small rectangles

Preparation

1. Fold and then roll each smoked salmon slice, gently opening its centre.
2. Place the lettuce in the centre of a plate. Display the avocado and grapefruit around the salad. Mix together the onions and chillies and place on top of the lettuce.
3. Mix the juice from the grapefruit with the cream and some black pepper. Add the chives. Drizzle on top and around the salad before serving.

Sun Temple – *Temple Soleil*

Pan-fried scallops with white onion, butter and lime, accompanied by a duo of peppers, with chicory endive and little gem lettuce, topped with olive oil

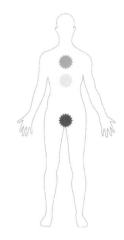

Ingredients

- 2 large scallops
- 300 millilitre milk, for soaking scallops
- salt to taste
- black pepper to taste
- 2 soup spoons olive oil
- 1 white onion, sliced
- 1/2 red pepper, sliced into equal shapes
- 1/2 yellow pepper, sliced into equal shapes
- 30 grams butter
- 1 head little gem lettuce, shredded
- 1 chicory endive, shredded
- squeeze of lemon juice

Preparation

1. Soak the scallops in milk with salt and pepper for 1 to 2 hours.
2. Heat the oil in a non-stick pan. Add the scallops, onion and peppers. Cook the scallops for 3 minutes on each side. When cooked, remove from heat and melt the butter on top.
3. Mix the lettuce and endive and place onto the plate. Display the scallop, onions and peppers on top. Sprinkle the melted butter around the salad.
4. Top with a squeeze of lime and black pepper and serve.

Coronation – *Couronnement*

Medley of white potato and anchovies with duo of black and white olives, enhanced with cherry tomatoes, boiled eggs, red onion, chives and coarse-grain mustard dressing

> ### The Message:
>
> *Welcome* the *abilities* within you towards *perseverance* and *discipline. Visualise* your life with *compassion.*

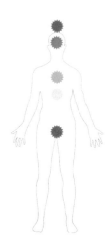

Ingredients

- 4 medium white potatoes, quartered
- 2 eggs
- 1 large red onion, thinly sliced
- 8 cherry tomatoes, quartered
- 14 black olives
- 14 white olives
- 10 chives, thinly sliced
- Salt to taste
- ground black pepper to taste
- 2 tea spoons coarse-grain mustard
- 6 soup spoons olive oil
- 2 soup spoons white wine vinegar
- 100 grams fresh anchovies

Preparation

1. Put the potatoes in a pan filled with cold water. Turn up the heat and once the water boils, check the potatoes and remove when ready. Let cool, then cut each quarter into halves or thirds (depending on potato size) and put in a bowl.
2. Boil the eggs for 10 minutes. Let cool, remove the shell and cut into 8 halved segments. Add to the bowl along with the onions, tomatoes, olives and chives. Add a pinch of salt and ground black pepper.
3. Prepare the dressing: Combine the mustard, olive oil and add salt and pepper. Mix well and add the vinegar. Once the dressing looks smooth, add to the main bowl and stir well.
4. When ready to serve, place on a plate and top with the fresh anchovies.

Note: Once the salad is prepared, you can eat it straight away or cover and place into the fridge for 24 hours to let the flavours infuse together.

The Trinity – *La Trinite*

Medley of salmon, cod fillets, squid and king prawns, with rice delicately flavoured with saffron, white onion, red and yellow peppers, garnished with parsley, fresh peas and tomato

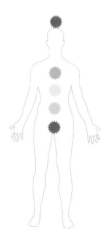

> ### The Message:
>
> Your *enlightened decision cleanses* your ego to give *birth* to *peace* within you. This *warm* feeling creates a *profusion* of *abundance*.

Ingredients

- 5 soup spoons olive oil or as needed
- 1 red pepper, thinly sliced
- 1 yellow pepper, thinly sliced
- 1 large white onion, thinly sliced
- 300g of long grain rice
- 1 large tomato, quartered
- 800 ml of vegetable or chicken stock
- 2 grams saffron
- 150 grams salmon fillet, cubed
- 150 grams cod loin, cubed
- 1 small squid, sliced into rings
- 12 raw king prawns, peeled
- 100 grams peas,
- parsley, chopped
- lemon wedge (optional)

Note: This dish can serve 4 and is delicious hot or cold.

Preparation

1. Cook with 3 soup spoons of olive oil the peppers and onions in a large frying pan. Remove when softened.
2. In the same pan, add 2 soup spoons of olive oil and cook the rice for 2 minutes.
3. Return the peppers and onions to the pan and add the tomato. Gradually pour some of the stock (300ml) into the pan and then add the saffron. Bring to a boil, reduce the heat and simmer for 12 minutes stirring regularly, adding more stock when needed.
4. Add the salmon, cod and squid with more stock if required and cook covered for another 8 minutes. Add the prawns, peas and more stock into the rice, stirring regularly. Cover and cook for a further 8 minutes.
5. Once there is little free liquid in the pan, serve garnished with chopped parsley. Add a lemon wedge if you wish.

MEAT AND EGG PLATES

Summer Solstice – *Solistice d'Ete*

Pan-fried medley of butternut squash, red potatoes, thyme and garlic with blanched sugar snap peas, lying on a bed of red leaf lettuce and topped with crispy bacon, hard-boiled eggs and mustard dressing

The Message:

Find *union* with *healing* within you and discover the *practice* of *conviviality*, *trust*, *attunement* and *understanding*.

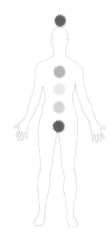

Ingredients

- 1/4 head red leaf lettuce
- 16 sugar snap peas
- 2 eggs
- 8 soup spoons olive oil
- 4 small red potatoes, washed and cut into eighths
- 1/2 small butternut squash, sliced in eighths long ways and then into triangles 5 centimetres thick
- 250 grams smoked bacon, thinly sliced
- 2 cloves garlic, peeled and thinly sliced
- 4 stems of thyme, chopped
- 1 tea spoon English mustard
- 2 soup spoons white wine vinegar

Preparation

1. Place the lettuce leaves on a plate.
2. Blanch the sugar snap peas for 3 minutes.
3. Boil the eggs for 10 minutes, let cool, peel and cut into 6 segments.
4. Heat 2 soup spoons of the olive oil in a pan. Add the potatoes, cover and cook over a medium heat, stirring occasionally until golden on each side, about 10 minutes. Add the butternut squash, cover and cook for 5 minutes. Add the bacon and cook for a further 5 minutes uncovered. Add the garlic and thyme to the pan and cook for a further 5 minutes.
5. Add the potato mixture and the egg segments to the salad.
6. In a bowl, combine the mustard with the remaining 6 soup spoons of olive oil and salt and pepper to taste. Add the vinegar and mix until a smooth consistency. Sprinkle the dressing onto the salad before serving.

Evolution – *Evolution*

Pan-fried chicken livers enhanced with garlic croutons, resting on a bed of little gem lettuce and asparagus with sunny cherry tomatoes and cucumber, flavoured with mustard dressing and parsley

The Message:

Persevere and *practice* your *kindness* to all and *embody* this *cleansing* act with *fluidity*.

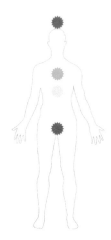

Ingredients

- 6 asparagus spears
- 1 slice bread
- 1 clove garlic, peeled
- 2 heads little gem lettuce
- 5 cherry tomatoes, halved
- 1/4 cucumber, sliced into half-moons
- 8 soup spoons olive oil
- 180 grams chicken livers
- 1 tea spoon English mustard
- 2 soup spoons white wine vinegar
- 2 stems of parsley, stems removed

Preparation

1. Blanch the asparagus in boiling water for 4 minutes and let cool.
2. Meanwhile, toast the bread. When it is toasted, rub the garlic on both sides and cut the bread into small squares.
3. Place the lettuce in the centre of a plate. Arrange the cherry tomatoes around the leaves. Place the cucumber slices evenly between the tomatoes. Sprinkle the toast squares over the salad.
4. Heat 2 soup spoons of olive oil. Add the chicken livers and cook to your taste. Place the cooked chicken livers on top of the salad.
5. Prepare the dressing: In a bowl, combine the mustard with the remaining 6 soup spoons of olive oil, hint of pepper and salt. Add the vinegar and mix until smooth. Sprinkle a soup spoon of the mixture all over the dish. Place the parsley leaves around the salad and serve.

Ease of Life – *Aisance de Vie*

Fan of duck breast with pineapple and ginger resting on curly leaf lettuce with freshly grated beetroot, seasoned with an orange jus

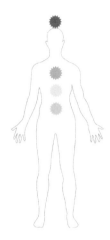

The Message:

When you are *willing*, the Universe *recognises* it and allows you to *master* these *sensations* and create with *ease*.

Ingredients

- 2 duck breasts (200 grams each)
- 40 grams ginger, chopped into fine batons
- juice from 1 orange
- 1 pineapple, peeled and sliced into rings, then quarters
- 1 raw beetroot, thinly grated
- 100 grams curly leaf lettuce

Preparation

1. Preheat oven to 180 degrees.
2. Heat a pan over a medium to high heat. Add the duck breasts fat-side down and sear for 4 minutes. Turn on the other side and cook for 1 minute more.
3. Place the duck in an oven-safe dish skin-side up. Add the ginger to the orange juice and pour over the duck. Top with the pineapple segments. Sprinkle some of the duck fat from the pan over the pineapple and cook in the oven for 10-15 minutes more.
4. Meanwhile, grate the beetroot thinly and leave it to dry out whilst cooking the duck.
5. Cut the cooked duck breast into 5 even slices.
6. Place the lettuce on a plate. Arrange the beetroot around the edge of the salad. Add the duck and pineapple. Sprinkle the juice from the baking pan all over before serving.

Appearance – *Apparition*

Nest of spinach and little gem lettuce, enhanced with fine beans, sliced shallots, crushed garlic and rosemary, garnished with red potatoes, sweet potato and cherry tomatoes, topped with poached eggs and dressed with sesame oil

The Message:

Persevere with the *healing* generated by *kindness*. It *creates* the *enthusiasm* to *appreciate* all life with *sensibility* and gives you the inner *patience* to *practice* with *determination* the love of all things.

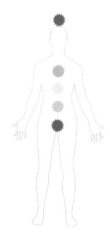

Ingredients

- 1 head little gem lettuce, sliced
- 80 grams spinach
- 100 grams fine beans
- 2 medium red potatoes, diced
- 1 large sweet potato, diced
- salt to taste
- pepper to taste
- 2 shallots, sliced
- 2 cloves garlic, crushed
- 6 cherry tomatoes, quartered
- 2 stems of rosemary, chopped
- 1 tea spoon white vinegar
- 2 eggs
- 6 soup spoons sesame oil
- 2 tea spoons honey

Preparation

1. Mix and place the lettuce with the spinach evenly onto the plate
2. Cook the beans in boiling water for 10 minutes. Cool under cold water. Place on the salad.
3. Cook with 2 soup spoons of sesame oil the red potatoes for 8 minutes then add the sweet potatoes, shallots, garlic and rosemary and cover for 8 minutes, stirring occasionally. Season to taste. Add the cherry tomatoes Remove from the heat when the tomatoes are slightly roasted. Add to the salad.
4. Boil hot water with the white vinegar in a pan. Crack open the eggs. Poach for 6 minutes before placing onto the salad.
5. Thinly sprinkle sesame oil around the dish. Pour the honey all over for your children's approval.

Sobriety – *Sobriete*

Refreshing medley of cucumber, tomato, celery and radishes, spinning around a heart of Chinese leaf lettuce and coriander, topped with grated carrot and enhanced with boiled eggs and a coarse-mustard lemon dressing

The Message:

Decide to *embody* your *beliefs* with *empathy*. They will become *trustworthy* and provide you the *balance, vitality,* and *light* of the Universe.

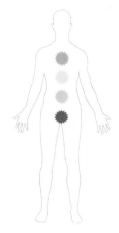

Ingredients

- 2 eggs
- 1/4 head Chinese leaf lettuce, thinly sliced
- 5 radishes, cut into halves
- 1 tomato, cut into 8 segments
- 1 celery stick, tip thinly cut
- 1/4 cucumber, sliced
- 1 carrot, grated
- 2 stems of coriander, stems removed
- 1/2 lemon squeezed
- 1 tea spoon coarse mustard
- 4 soup spoons olive oil

Preparation

1. Plunge the eggs into boiling water for 10 minutes. Cool under cold water, remove shell and slice into 6 segments.
2. Place the lettuce in the centre of a plate. Arrange the egg segments around the salad.
3. Cut the radishes into stars: Insert a pointy knife diagonally in the middle of the radish to create a series of linked 'V' cuts all around and then open up. Add to the plate.
4. Add the tomato, celery, cucumber, carrot, coriander and a squeeze of lemon juice to the salad.
5. In a bowl, combine in the following order, the mustard, salt, pepper and olive oil. Add the lemon juice and mix to obtain a smooth consistency. Sprinkle on the salad and serve.

Gentle Force – *Force Douce*

Warm duck liver resting with pan-fried white potato slices on a bed of romaine lettuce, flavoured with dried prunes, sultanas and white onion

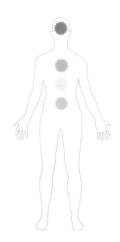

The Message:

The *prowess* of your actions gives *birth* to *flexibility* and *discipline* in reaching your *vision*.

Ingredients

- 2 medium white potatoes
- 3 soup spoons olive oil
- 160 grams duck liver
- 20 millilitres water
- 1 white onion, thinly sliced
- 40 grams sultanas, soaked in hot water
- 6 dried prunes, pitted
- 1/4 head romaine lettuce, prepared

Preparation

1. Cook the potatoes in cold water for 15 minutes. Cool and cut lengthways into slices.
2. Heat 2 spoons of olive oil in a pan. Add the potatoes and cook until golden crisp on both sides. Remove the potatoes from the pan and set aside.
3. Add 1 soup spoon of olive oil to the pan and cook the liver for 5 minutes and add the onion. When nicely coloured on both sides, add the sultanas and dried prunes with a small amount of water. Let simmer until the juice reduces slightly.
4. Display the lettuce, potatoes and liver mixture on a plate. Sprinkle the cooking juices on top.

Milky Way – *Voie Lactee*

Crispy bacon, green lentils and red onion resting on spinach leaves, topped with new potatoes, carrots and leek, flavoured with freshly chopped parsley and mustard dressing

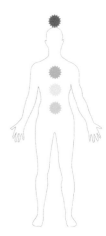

The Message:

Discipline and *friendliness* towards others gives you the *ability* to *cleanse* yourself, and *determines* the intense *generosity* and *vitality* within you.

Ingredients

- 180 grams green lentils, washed
- 2 carrots
- 4 new potatoes
- 1 leek, sliced into rings
- 100 grams bacon, thinly cut
- 4 stems of parsley, chopped
- 1 red onion, diced
- 2 tea spoons mustard
- 6 soup spoons olive oil
- 2 soup spoons white wine vinegar
- 60 grams spinach leaves

Preparation

1. Cook the lentils in boiling water until tender. Place in a large bowl.
2. Cook the carrots and potatoes from cold water for 20–25 minutes. Add the leek for the last 5 minutes of cooking. Let cool and then slice the carrots and potatoes lengthways into quarters. Add the carrots, potatoes and leek to the bowl.
3. Cook the bacon in a pan over a medium heat until crispy. Add to the bowl along with the parsley and red onion.
4. In a bowl, combine the mustard, olive oil and a pinch of salt and pepper. Add the vinegar and mix well to obtain a smooth consistency. Pour over in the main bowl and stir well.
5. Display the salad mixture on a nest of spinach leaves when ready to eat.

Note: You can eat the salad warm or place it in the fridge for a few hours to let the flavours mix before serving.

Seduction – *Seduction*

Refreshing seared honey-coated chicken supreme with fennel, delicately placed on a bed of arugula salad, with a fan of avocado and peach, enhanced with fresh coriander seeds

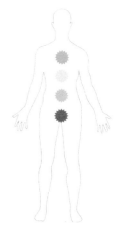

The Message:

Align yourself to connect to the *knowledge* and *loveliness* within you. It is filled with *empathy* and *delight*.

Ingredients

- 2 soup spoons olive oil
- 2 chicken fillets
- 1 head fennel, thinly sliced
- 3 tea spoons clear honey
- 20 coriander seeds
- 150 grams arugula salad
- 1 avocado, sliced
- 1 peach, sliced
- 30 millilitre water
- 2 coriander stems

Preparation

1. Heat 2 soup spoons of olive oil in a pan. Add the chicken and sear for 2 minutes on each side. Add the fennel and cook for 4 minutes more.
2. Mix the honey with some hot water and the coriander seeds. Pour over the hot dish. Cover and simmer for another 8 minutes.
3. Arrange the arugula leaves on the plate. Fan the avocado and peach slices to display on top of the arugula.
4. Place the cooked chicken and fennel on top of the salad and sprinkle the cooking juices over the top.
5. Garnish with coriander leaves and serve.

Synchronisation – *Synchronisation*

Seared fillet of pork with pink lady and cooking apples served with red lentils, lamb lettuce and thyme, enhanced with dried prunes and walnut oil

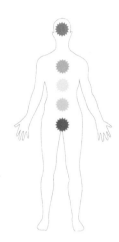

Ingredients

- 150 grams red lentils
- 3 stems of thyme, chopped
- 2 soup spoons walnut oil, plus more for drizzling
- 200 grams pork fillet
- 1 cooking apple, cut into equal segments
- 1 pink lady apple, cut into equal segments
- 80 grams lamb lettuce
- 12 dried prunes, halved

Preparation

1. Wash and cook the lentils in boiling water until tender. Top with thyme and a drizzle of walnut oil.
2. Heat the 2 soup spoons of walnut oil in a pan. Add the pork and sear covered for 6 minutes on each side or until cooked through. Remove from the heat and place the fillet in a dish. Cover with foil.
3. Add the pink lady apple to the pan and cook over a medium heat for 1 minute each side or until softened. Repeat with the cooking apples.
4. Arrange the lettuce on a plate. Display the other ingredients atop the lettuce, finishing with the prunes.
5. Drizzle with walnut oil and serve.

FRESH FRUIT PLATES

Harmony – *Harmonie*

Perfect formation of pomegranate pods, banana circles, peach segments, mango slices, pineapple pieces and honeydew melon triangles

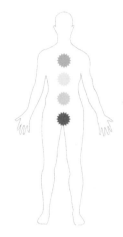

The Message:

You have the *connection* of *being* in *delight* with the *recognition* and *beauty* of your *autonomy*.

Ingredients

- 1 pomegranate, separated into pods
- 1 peach, cut into segments
- 1 banana, cut into circles
- 1 mango, sliced
- 1 pineapple, cut into pieces
- 1/4 honeydew melon, cut into triangles

Preparation

1. First place the mango, followed by the melon then the pineapple.
2. Add the banana on top, the peach segments around and finish with the pomegranate.

Illumination – *Illumination*

Refreshing raspberries, orange and honeydew melon, crowned with green gooseberries, blueberries, blackcurrants, cherries and mint

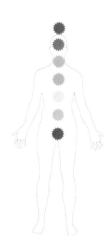

The Message:

Your *presence inspires* and *transmits modest sensations* to *empower* and *reflect* on every *being*.

Ingredients

- 10 raspberries
- 1 orange, separated into segments
- 1/4 melon, cut into half segments
- 6 gooseberries, quartered
- 14 blackcurrants, halved
- 4 cherries, pitted and quartered
- 18 blueberries
- 2 sprigs of mint, stems removed

Preparation

1. Start from the base of the plate with the raspberries and work your way up with the oranges, melon, gooseberries, blueberries, blackcurrants and cherries.
2. Place the fresh mint into a blueberry and arrange in the middle of the plate.

Sunshine – *Ensoleillement*

Delightful combination of persimmon (sharon fruit), oranges and satsuma segments, enlaced with full- and quarter-moon red grapes

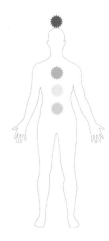

The Message:

A new *sensation transforms* your *dynamism* towards *spiritual wealth.*

Ingredients

- 2 persimmons, cut into 8 segments
- 2 oranges, separated into segments
- 2 satsumas, separated into segments
- 16 red grapes, whole
- 4 red grapes, quartered

Preparation

1. Display the satsuma segments in a circle on the middle of the plate.
2. Place the orange segments between the satsuma gaps. Add the whole grapes between the orange segments, followed by the persimmon segments.
3. Surround with the grapes quartered in between the persimmon.

Simplicity – *Simplicite*

Medley of ripe summer fruits, including strawberries, raspberries, redcurrants, gooseberries, blackcurrants, cherries, black plums and red grapes, enhanced with fresh mint

The Message:

The *transmission* and *reflection* of your *love empowers* with *modesty* and *proficiency,* the *resources* to the *presence* of endless *wealth* in many shapes and forms.

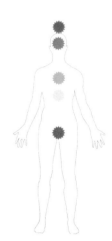

Ingredients

- 4 strawberries, whole
- 2 black plums, halved and pitted
- 10 raspberries
- 16 red grapes
- 14 blackcurrants
- 2 bunches of redcurrants, stems removed
- 8 gooseberries
- 6 cherries, pitted (optional)
- 2 sprigs of mint

Preparation

1. Display the fruits onto each plate to your liking.

Abundance - *Abondance*

Beautiful circle of watermelon, dancing with raspberries and strawberries, topped with redcurrants and pink grapefruit segments

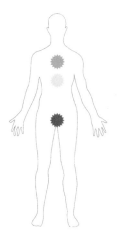

The Message:

Through *love*, you have the *resources* to stay *grounded* and *empower* your *energy* on earth.

Ingredients

- 1/4 watermelon, cut into equal triangles
- 10 raspberries
- 1 pink grapefruit, separated into segments
- 2 strawberries quartered, then halved
- 2 bunches of redcurrants, with stems

Preparation

1. Place the 7 watermelon pieces around the plate evenly. Add the strawberry segments in between each triangle to create a circle.
2. Place the raspberries in the middle, the grapefruit on top of every other water melon triangle and the redcurrants on the remaining triangles.

Balance – *Equilibre*

Circle of freshly sliced apricots, black plums, nectarines, strawberries and kiwis, surrounded with blueberries and red grapes

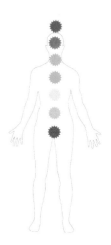

The Message:

Your *proficiency* is *amazing* and unleashes *goodwill* within you. It is a *wealth* of *happiness inspired* through *unconditional love.*

Ingredients

- 1 apricot, pitted and sliced
- 16 blueberries
- 1 black plum, pitted and sliced
- 2 strawberries, sliced
- 1 nectarine, sliced
- 2 kiwis, sliced
- 4 red grapes, quartered

Preparation

1. Place the sliced kiwi in the middle of the plate and surround with the other fruits into a fan.
2. Finish by placing evenly the quartered grapes and blueberries around the circle of fruits.

Polarity - *Polarite*

Symphony of blueberries, red grapes, cherries, blackcurrants and plums

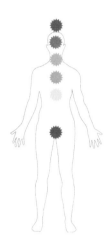

The Message:

Your spiritual and material
wealth reflect and *inspire* many
to generate *proficient* happiness
to everyone surrounding you.

Ingredients

- 1 punnet of blueberries
- 6 cherries, pitted (optional)
- 2 black plums, pitted (optional)
- 10 red grapes, whole
- 12 blackcurrants

Preparation

1. After washing the fruits, place 1 blueberry on the middle of the plate and create a cross with the remaining berries.
2. Place each other fruit in each section as per the picture, or to your inspiration of the moment.

Flamboyance – *Flamboyance*

Fan of cantaloupe melon with pear and mandarin segments, sliced banana and strawberries with white grapes

The Message:

You feel *secure,* allowing you to *connect* with your *love spontaneity.* This *dynamism* generates *a new* you.

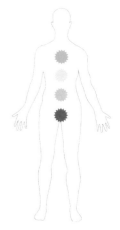

Ingredients

- 1/2 cantaloupe melon, sliced thinly into segments, then halved
- 1 pear, cut into segments
- 1 banana, sliced
- 1 mandarin, separated into segments
- 6 strawberries, quartered
- 2 strawberries, whole
- 8 white grapes, halved

Preparation

1. Place a whole strawberry in the centre of the plate.
2. Create an inner circle with the fan of melon with each tip edging the plate and add banana into the circle and the grapes in between the melon tip.
3. Lay the pear slices from the strawberry on top of the banana to create a flower. Add the mandarin segments and the quartered strawberries in the centre of the plate.

Universal Will – *Volonte Universelle*

Trio of kiwis, red grapes and orange segments, dancing with blueberries, blackberries and figs

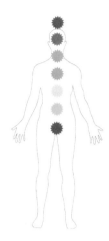

Ingredients

- 2 kiwis, cut into 8 segments
- 12 red grapes, 2 whole and the others quartered
- 14 blueberries
- 1 punnet of blackberries
- 2 oranges, separated into segments
- 2 figs, quartered

Preparation

1. Create a circle with the quartered grapes in the middle of the plate. Add in between the oranges, then the kiwis.
2. Surround with the figs, blackberries and grapes as per the picture.
3. Top with the whole grape and blueberries.

Love Flake – *Flocon d'Amour*

Medallions of strawberries, blackberries, cherries, raspberries, redcurrants and blueberries combined into Oneness

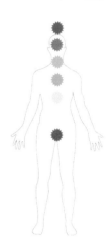

The Message:

Your *reflection* and *transmission* of *love* is *resourceful* and *empowers* others to be *inspired*.

Ingredients

- 10 raspberries
- 6 strawberries, (2 whole, 4 quartered)
- 10 cherries
- 20 blueberries
- 1 punnet of blackberries
- 10 bunches of redcurrants with stems

Preparation

1. Place a whole strawberry in the middle of the plate. Surround with the blackberries and add alternatively the cherries and raspberries.
2. Add the quartered strawberries atop each raspberry and place a blueberry each side of the strawberry. Finish with the redcurrants in between the blueberries.

Angelic Dance – *Dance Angelique*

Delicate segments of pink and white grapefruit, oranges, kiwis and limes dancing in harmony

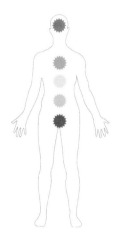

The Message:

With *assertiveness, fuse* your *senses* to be *amazed* by the *energy* within you.

Ingredients

- 1 pink grapefruit, separated into segments, halved
- 1 white grapefruit, separated into segments, halved
- 1 kiwi, sliced and quartered
- 2 limes, separated into segments
- 2 oranges, separated into segments

Preparation

1. Start by placing 3 half white grapefruit segments in the middle of the plate and 3 orange segments between the gaps. Add 2 more white grapefruit segments between the orange and surround with the kiwis.
2. Surround with the remaining 6 oranges in pairs, evenly apart. Add the lime segments and the red grapefruit in between each gap.

Heaven Garden - *Jardin du Paradis*

Refined medley of apricots, kiwi, black plums and strawberries in fusion with blackberries, white grapes and mint

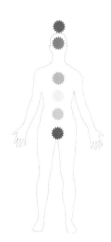

The Message:

With *proficiency* and
perception, your *presence*
generates *amazement* towards
happiness and *love anew*
for everyone to receive.

Ingredients

- 3 apricots, halved and pitted
- 2 black plums, thickly sliced
- 6 strawberries
- 8 blackberries
- 1 kiwi, peeled and halved
- 8 white grapes, quartered
- 12 mint leaves

Preparation

1. Remove the skin of the kiwi then cut into stars: Insert a pointy knife diagonally in the middle of the kiwi to create a series of linked 'V' cuts all around and then open up.
2. Place the other fruit on the plate as per the picture or per your inspiration.

Mindful Practice

Whatever you do, always try to look for an uplifting perspective to any situation.

"When it is going "great", enjoy it! When it is getting challenging, observe it! As everything, it will pass ... Being the observer instead of the actor, allows you to fly through these times with ease and encourages peace within."

Consciously create a desired vibration

Use the 'A to Z Guide' that follows to select the vibration you wish to generate within you for the day or week. This can relate to healing a health issue, boosting a joyful state of mind, creating a state of well-being, resolving a challenging situation or connecting with your inner self.

'I am' consciousness practice

Refer to the 'A to Z Guide' for the meaning of all the ingredients you are planning to eat for the day. Write them down on a piece of paper. Then, as you breathe out, repeat the 'I am + meaning' statement, and as you breathe in, the 'I am', five times for each ingredient that you will eat. Focus on the meaning, vibration and related chakra.

Let your intuition speak to you

Check out the meanings of the ingredients you shop for each week. Notice how the meanings of the produce you have purchased coincides with your current situation, thoughts or state of mind – and how they can help you achieve your desired vibration.

Inspire your children to assemble the fruit platters

Once you have done the cutting preparation, involve your children to create the plates with you. You can ask them to follow the step by step preparation and be guided from the picture of the platter, or let them use their inspiration to create their own masterpiece before savouring it together.

A to Z Guide to Fruits and Vegetables
Meaning, Vibration and Related Chakras

Almond
- *Meaning*: inner truth
- *Vibration*: allow to relate deeper within
- *Related chakras*: solar plexus and sacral

Apple, cooking
- *Meaning*: sympathy
- *Vibration*: ability to understand and share somebody else's feelings
- *Related chakras*: heart, solar plexus and root

Apple, green
- *Meaning*: joy
- *Vibration*: connection towards happiness within
- *Related chakras*: heart and solar plexus

Apple, pink lady
- *Meaning*: contribution
- *Vibration*: allow the achievement of something towards self or others
- *Related chakras*: heart, solar plexus and root

Apple, red
- *Meaning*: passion
- *Vibration*: enthusiasm or intense emotion to make manifest something
- *Related chakras*: heart, solar plexus and root

Apricot
- *Meaning*: happiness
- *Vibration*: enhance providential recovery towards happy outcomes
- *Related chakras*: solar plexus, sacral and root

Arugula (rocket) leaves

- *Meaning*: alignment
- *Vibration*: integration and harmonisation with the soul
- *Related chakras*: heart

Asparagus

- *Meaning*: fluidity
- *Vibration*: welcoming the flow of life
- *Related chakras*: crown, heart and solar plexus

Aubergine (eggplant)

- *Meaning*: proficiency
- *Vibration*: elevation of personal awareness
- *Related chakras*: crown, third eye and solar plexus

Avocado

- *Meaning*: knowledge
- *Vibration*: certainty to have the truths and principles within
- *Related chakras*: heart and solar plexus

Banana

- *Meaning*: connection
- *Vibration*: connects with ease to sensations, feelings, inner self
- *Related chakras*: solar plexus

Basil

- *Meaning*: freshness
- *Vibration*: new to one's experience, revived, reinvigorated
- *Related chakras*: heart

Beans, fine/French

- *Meaning*: sensibility
- *Vibration*: feel and perceive uplifting vibrations
- *Related chakras*: heart

Beetroot

- *Meaning*: mastery
- *Vibration*: allow complete understanding and clarity
- *Related chakras*: crown

Blackberry

- *Meaning*: perception
- *Vibration*: connect with insight and intuition
- *Related chakras*: third eye

Blackcurrant

- *Meaning*: reflection
- *Vibration*: manifestation of a new and uplifting perspective
- *Related chakras*: third eye

Blueberry

- *Meaning*: inspiration
- *Vibration*: divine guidance exerted directly on the mind from the soul
- *Related chakras*: third eye, throat and heart

Broccoli

- *Meaning*: offering
- *Vibration*: allow kind contribution to self and others
- *Related chakras*: heart and solar plexus

Butternut squash

- *Meaning*: union
- *Vibration*: ability to harmonise situations and self
- *Related chakras*: sacral

Carrot

- *Meaning*: vitality
- *Vibration*: generate positive and creative energy
- *Related chakras*: sacral

Cashew nuts

- *Meaning*: grace
- *Vibration*: generosity of spirit – elegance, beauty and smoothness of movement of self
- *Related chakras*: sacral

Celery

- *Meaning*: balance
- *Vibration*: bring satisfying and harmonious wholeness
- *Related chakras*: heart and solar plexus

Cherry, black

- *Meaning*: transmission
- *Vibration*: expression of light or sound from divine energy
- *Related chakras*: crown

Chicory endive, white

- *Meaning*: wisdom
- *Vibration*: sense and expression shown with unconditional love and without judgment
- *Related chakras*: heart and solar plexus

Chilli, red

- *Meaning*: ease
- *Vibration*: freedom from difficulty, hardship or effort
- *Related chakras*: root

Chinese leaf

- *Meaning*: belief
- *Vibration*: confidence, certainty of the manifestation
- *Related chakras*: heart and solar plexus

Chive

- *Meaning*: welcoming
- *Vibration*: to receive and accept with joy
- *Related chakras*: heart

Clementine

- *Meaning*: pleasure
- *Vibration*: source of enjoyment and delight towards gratification of 'being'
- *Related chakras*: sacral

Coriander

- *Meaning*: empathy
- *Vibration*: power of understanding and imaginatively holding space for another person
- *Related chakras*: heart

Courgette (zucchini)

- *Meaning*: availability
- *Vibration*: willingness to serve, be of service
- *Related chakras*: heart and solar plexus

Cranberry

- *Meaning*: harvest
- *Vibration*: receive the fruits of your work
- *Related chakras*: solar plexus and root

Cucumber

- *Meaning*: embodiment
- *Vibration*: to make manifest, give tangible and definite form to intention
- *Related chakras*: heart and solar plexus

Eggplant (aubergine)

- *Meaning*: proficiency
- *Vibration*: elevation of personal awareness
- *Related chakras*: crown, third eye and solar plexus

Fennel

- *Meaning*: loveliness
- *Vibration*: expressing beauty
- *Related chakras*: heart and solar plexus

Fig

- *Meaning*: evolution
- *Vibration*: ability for growth and development through willingness to change
- *Related chakras*: crown, heart, solar plexus and root

Garlic

- *Meaning*: practice
- *Vibration*: act with consistency and complete awareness
- *Related chakras*: solar plexus

Ginger

- *Meaning*: willingness
- *Vibration*: act gladly
- *Related chakras*: solar plexus

Gooseberry, green

- *Meaning*: modesty
- *Vibration*: humility towards your achievement and abilities
- *Related chakras*: heart and solar plexus

Grape, red

- *Meaning*: wealth
- *Vibration*: abundance manifesting in many shapes and forms
- *Related chakras*: crown and heart

Grape, white

- *Meaning*: anew
- *Vibration*: being in a new way that is uplifting from the previous one
- *Related chakras*: heart and solar plexus

Grapefruit, pink

- *Meaning*: energy
- *Vibration*: intensify the action or expression
- *Related chakras*: root

Grapefruit, white

- *Meaning*: assertiveness
- *Vibration*: generate certainty, acceptance, affirmation, confidence within
- *Related chakras*: solar plexus

Hazelnut

- *Meaning*: health
- *Vibration*: general soundness, vitality and proper functioning of body, mind and spirit
- *Related chakras*: solar plexus and sacral

Kiwi

- *Meaning*: amazement
- *Vibration*: amplify the state of wonder
- *Related chakras*: third eye, heart and solar plexus

Leek

- *Meaning*: friendliness
- *Vibration*: being affectionate, trusting, helpful towards self or another
- *Related chakras*: heart and solar plexus

Lemon

- *Meaning*: light
- *Vibration*: enhance inspiration and spiritual awareness
- *Related chakras*: solar plexus

Lentil, green

- *Meaning*: generosity
- *Vibration*: activate self-recognition of abundance and fullness
- *Related chakras*: heart

Lentil, red

- *Meaning*: satisfaction
- *Vibration*: assurance beyond doubt of fulfilment, contentment and gratification
- *Related chakras*: sacral

Lettuce, Batavia

- *Meaning*: freedom
- *Vibration*: ability to be authentic, without being subject to undue restraints or restrictions
- *Related chakras*: heart

Lettuce, cos

- *Meaning*: affection
- *Vibration*: disposition to feel and send fondness towards self or another person
- *Related chakras*: heart and solar plexus

Lettuce, curly/frisée

- *Meaning*: attraction
- *Vibration*: magnetic force that draws togetherness and pleasure
- *Related chakras*: heart and solar plexus

Lettuce, lamb

- *Meaning*: calm
- *Vibration*: being serene, tranquil, at peace
- *Related chakras*: heart

Lettuce, little gem

- *Meaning*: kindness
- *Vibration*: act with compassion
- *Related chakras*: heart and solar plexus

Lettuce, oak leaf

- *Meaning*: contemplation
- *Vibration*: trustful reflection towards an intention
- *Related chakras*: crown and heart

Lettuce, red leaf

- *Meaning*: understanding
- *Vibration*: sympathetically aware of feelings; expressing tolerance and forgiveness
- *Related chakras*: crown, heart and solar plexus

Lettuce, romaine
- *Meaning*: flexibility
- *Vibration*: ability to welcome change with trust and confidence
- *Related chakras*: heart and solar plexus

Lettuce, round
- *Meaning*: fineness
- *Vibration*: feeling clean and pure
- *Related chakras*: heart

Lime
- *Meaning*: fusion
- *Vibration*: create by merging the thoughts and the emotions
- *Related chakras*: heart

Mandarin
- *Meaning*: dynamism
- *Vibration*: universal force that generates the energy of creation
- *Related chakras*: sacral

Mango
- *Meaning*: beauty
- *Vibration*: outstanding example of its kind, all qualities expressed within and around
- *Related chakras*: solar plexus and sacral

Melon, cantaloupe
- *Meaning*: spontaneity
- *Vibration*: expressing awareness from the heart and soul
- *Related chakras*: sacral

Melon, honeydew
- *Meaning*: being
- *Vibration*: expressing the essence of love, peace and joy
- *Related chakras*: solar plexus and heart

Mint

- *Meaning*: presence
- *Vibration*: physical manifestation of the spirit in self
- *Related chakras*: heart

Nectarine

- *Meaning*: goodwill
- *Vibration*: allow kindness towards self or another
- *Related chakras*: solar plexus and root chakras

Olive, black

- *Meaning*: visualisation
- *Vibration*: generate visual perception of an intention, action or dream
- *Related chakras*: third eye

Olive, green

- *Meaning*: compassion
- *Vibration*: hold presence and awareness towards self or others with the intention to relieve it
- *Related chakras*: heart

Olive oil

- *Meaning*: trust
- *Vibration*: create confidence and certainty within self
- *Related chakras*: solar plexus

Onion, red

- *Meaning*: ability
- *Vibration*: trust the possibility to create anything
- *Related chakras*: crown and solar plexus

Onion, spring

- *Meaning*: youth
- *Vibration*: express from the heart, limitless trust
- *Related chakras*: heart and solar plexus

Onion, white
- *Meaning*: birth
- *Vibration*: allow old thoughts, states and situations to make space for new uplifting ones
- *Related chakras*: solar plexus

Orange
- *Meaning*: sensation
- *Vibration*: feel and perceive with our sixth sense
- *Related chakras*: sacral

Orange, blood
- *Meaning*: rhapsody
- *Vibration*: enable the feeling that creates elated bliss
- *Related chakras*: crown, sacral and root

Parsley
- *Meaning*: cleansing
- *Vibration*: act of purification, ability to remove guilt, worry, doubt
- *Related chakras*: heart

Peach
- *Meaning*: delight
- *Vibration*: expression of pure joy
- *Related chakras*: solar plexus, sacral and root

Pear
- *Meaning*: security
- *Vibration*: enhanced self-confidence; freedom from doubt, anxiety or fear
- *Related chakras*: solar plexus and heart.

Peas
- *Meaning*: abundance
- *Vibration*: self-realisation of fullness in every shape and form
- *Related chakras*: heart

Pepper, green
- *Meaning*: radiance
- *Vibration*: generate the brightness of light
- *Related chakras*: heart

Pepper orange
- *Meaning*: expression
- *Vibration*: generate feeling of the manifestation of an intention
- *Related chakras*: sacral

Pepper, red
- *Meaning*: warmth
- *Vibration*: provide affection and kindness through love expression
- *Related chakras*: root

Pepper, yellow
- *Meaning*: enlightened
- *Vibration*: radiate light upon self or another
- *Related chakras*: solar plexus

Persimmon (sharon fruit)
- *Meaning*: transformation
- *Vibration*: act to change
- *Related chakras*: sacral

Pineapple
- *Meaning*: recognition
- *Vibration*: allow the perception of truth – realisation, acceptance and acknowledgment
- *Related chakras*: solar plexus

Plum, black
- *Meaning*: proficient
- *Vibration*: provide great facility and skilful ability
- *Related chakras*: third eye, solar plexus and root

Pomegranate
- *Meaning*: autonomy
- *Vibration*: independence and freedom of your being
- *Related chakras*: solar plexus and root

Potato, red
- *Meaning*: healing
- *Vibration*: activate the effect of curing or improving
- *Related chakras*: solar plexus and root

Potato, sweet
- *Meaning*: enthusiasm
- *Vibration*: create excitement and confidence towards an inspiration or belief
- *Related chakras*: sacral and root

Potato, white/new
- *Meaning*: discipline
- *Vibration*: practice with consistency, focus and awareness
- *Related chakras*: solar plexus

Prunes
- *Meaning*: vision
- *Vibration*: allow discernment or perception through self-awareness
- *Related chakras*: third eye

Pumpkin seeds
- *Meaning*: clarity
- *Vibration*: receive with certainty, transparency and inspiration from the soul
- *Related chakras*: heart and solar plexus

Radish
- *Meaning*: trustworthy
- *Vibration*: confirmation of trust and confidence
- *Related chakras*: solar plexus and root

Raisins
- *Meaning*: intuition
- *Vibration*: connect to inner knowledge
- *Related chakras*: third eye

Raspberry
- *Meaning*: empowerment
- *Vibration*: enhance the ability to 'be', the highest expression of self
- *Related chakras*: root

Redcurrant
- *Meaning*: resourceful
- *Vibration*: generate ingenuity and capability to deal promptly with new situations
- *Related chakras*: root chakra

Rice
- *Meaning*: peace
- *Vibration*: encourage inner contentment and serenity
- *Related chakras*: solar plexus and sacral

Rosemary
- *Meaning*: creativity
- *Vibration*: ability to use own imagination to develop new and original outcomes
- *Related chakras*: heart and solar plexus

Saffron
- *Meaning*: profusion
- *Vibration*: self-realisation of fullness in every shape and form
- *Related chakras*: solar plexus and sacral

Satsuma
- *Meaning*: dynamism
- *Vibration*: universal force that generates the energy of creation
- *Related chakras*: sacral

Sesame oil
- *Meaning*: appreciation
- *Vibration*: express gratitude and recognition
- *Related chakras*: sacral

Shallots
- *Meaning*: patience
- *Vibration*: being calm, tolerant and trusting
- *Related chakras*: crown and solar plexus

Sharon fruit (persimmon)
- *Meaning*: transformation
- *Vibration*: act to change
- *Related chakras*: sacral

Spinach
- *Meaning*: determination
- *Vibration*: activate resolution and consistency towards an action
- *Related chakras*: heart

Strawberry
- *Meaning*: love
- *Vibration*: express deep, tender, ineffable and unconditional feeling; enlightenment
- *Related chakras*: heart, solar plexus and root

Sugar snap peas
- *Meaning*: conviviality
- *Vibration*: being of a joyful expression
- *Related chakras*: heart

Sultanas
- *Meaning*: prowess
- *Vibration*: provide superior inner strength, courage and confidence in self
- *Related chakras*: solar plexus and sacral

Sweetcorn

- *Meaning*: quality
- *Vibration*: Encourage self-excellence to manifest
- *Related chakras*: solar plexus

Tarragon

- *Meaning*: vibration
- *Vibration*: allow your body to send and receive the energy of the moment
- *Related chakras*: heart

Thyme

- *Meaning*: attunement
- *Vibration*: bring accord and harmony
- *Related chakras*: heart

Tomato

- *Meaning*: decision
- *Vibration*: act to be determinate and authentic with self
- *Related chakras*: solar plexus and root

Tomato, cherry

- *Meaning*: perseverance
- *Vibration*: trust in the action of grace
- *Related chakras*: solar plexus and root

Walnut oil/walnuts

- *Meaning*: optimism
- *Vibration*: confidence and positivity; see the best outcome
- *Related chakras*: solar plexus and sacral

Watermelon

- *Meaning*: grounded
- *Vibration*: anchored onto Mother Earth
- *Related chakras*: third eye and root

Zucchini (courgette)

- *Meaning*: availability
- *Vibration*: willingness to serve
- *Related chakras*: heart and solar plexus

Resources

Chakras

➢ Deanna M. Minich, Ph.D., C.N., *The Complete Handbook of Quantum Healing: An A-Z Self-Healing Guide for Over 100 Common Ailments* (Conari Press Wellness, 2010)

➢ New Age Spirituality (http://new-age-spirituality.com, select the colour section)

Colours – meaning

➢ William Berton, *Colours Energy book & chart* (Colorscope Press, 2007), http://www.telling-colours.co.uk/ .Select "Telling colours".

➢ Colours: Colour Meaning for Magic, Healing and Enhancing Your Life' http://www.alizons-psychic-secrets.com/colours.html

Fruits and vegetable colour reference

➢ http://www.sanitarium.com.au/health-and-wellbeing/colour-me-healthy

Printed in the United States
By Bookmasters